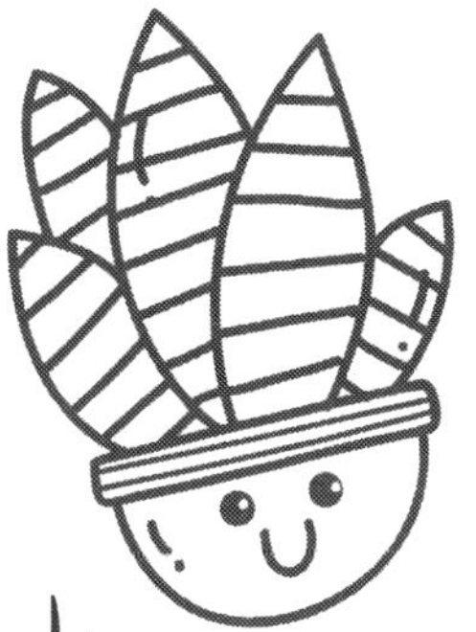

Kawaii Cactus Coloring Book

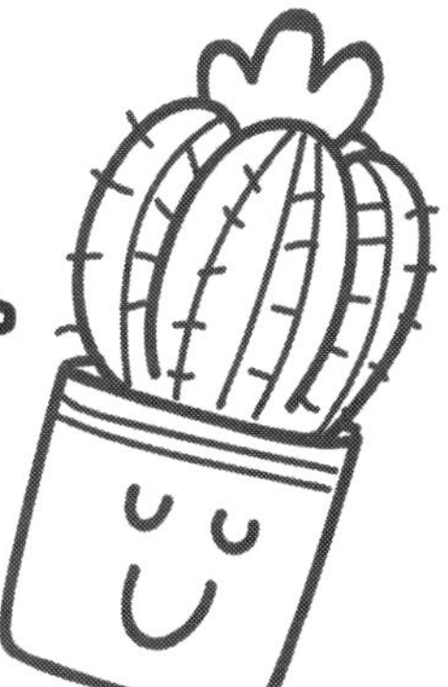

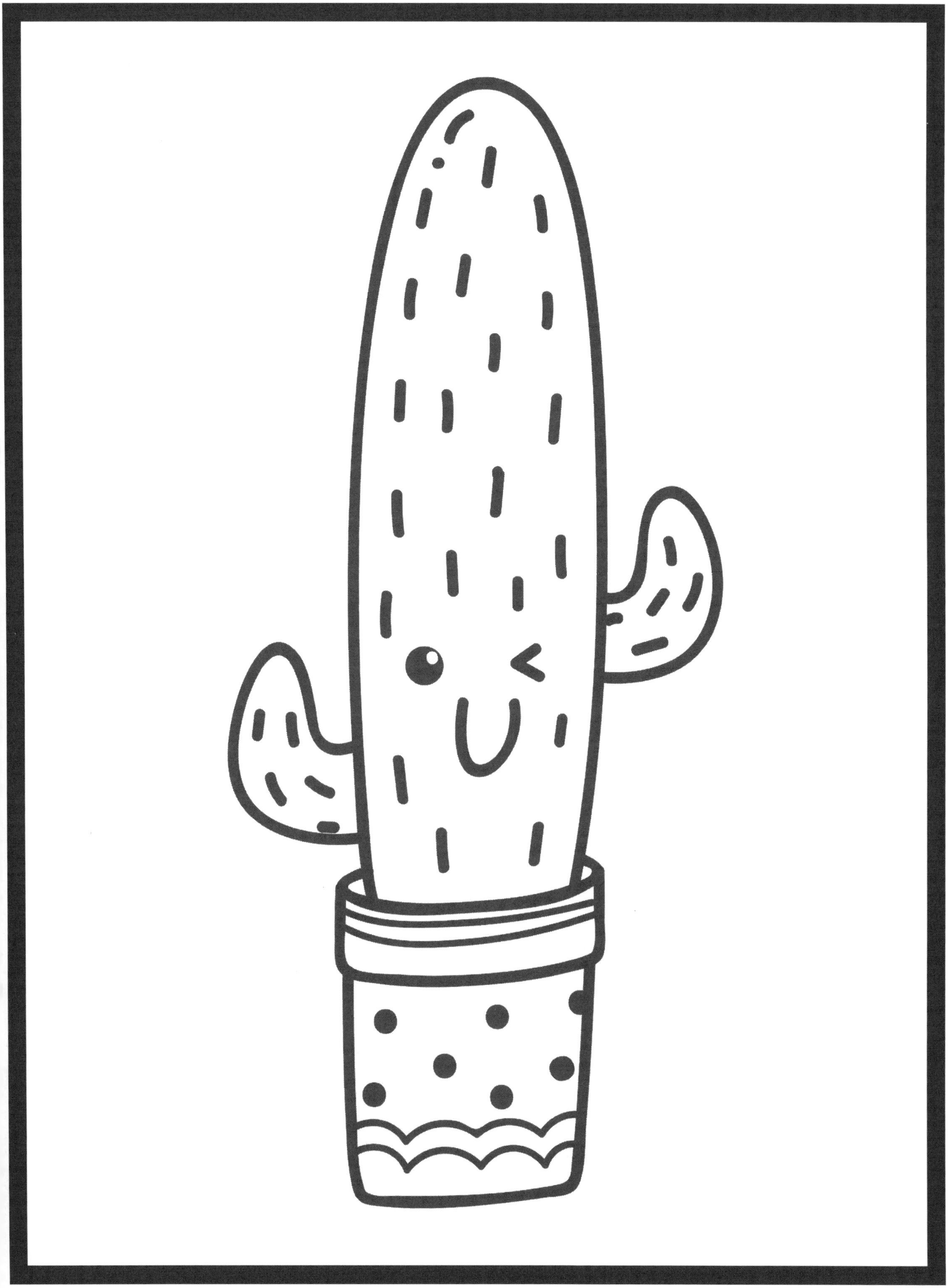

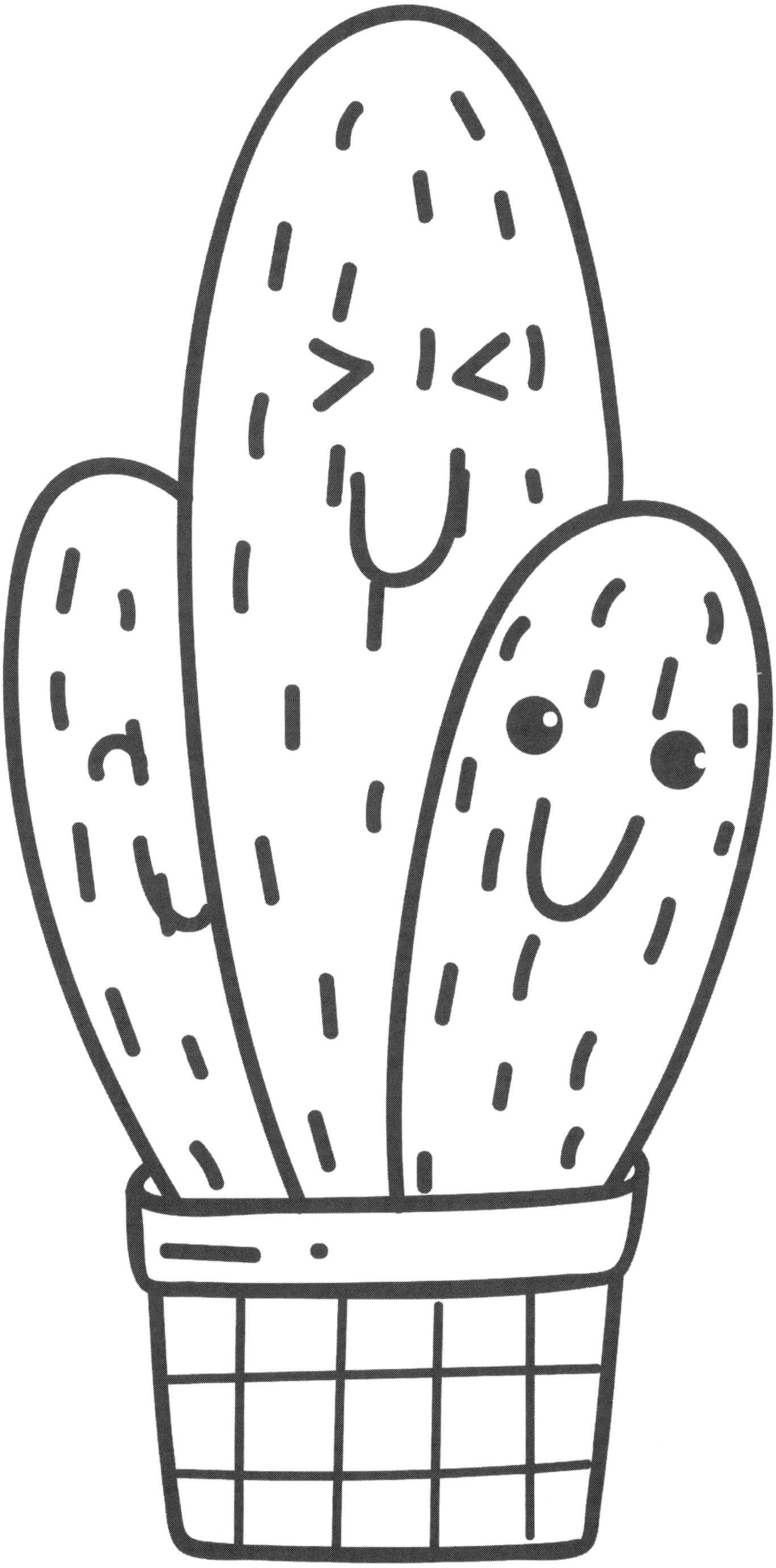

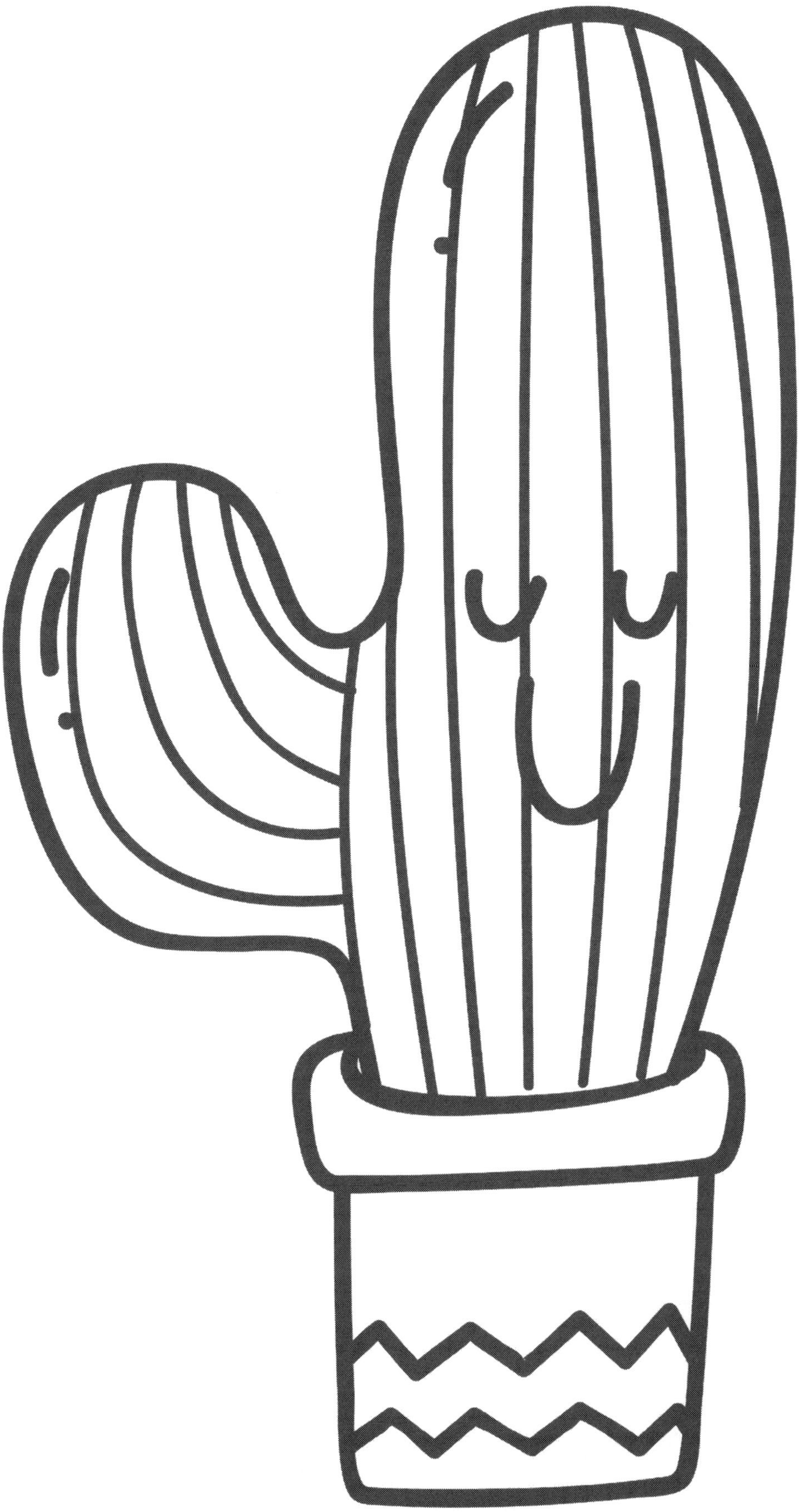

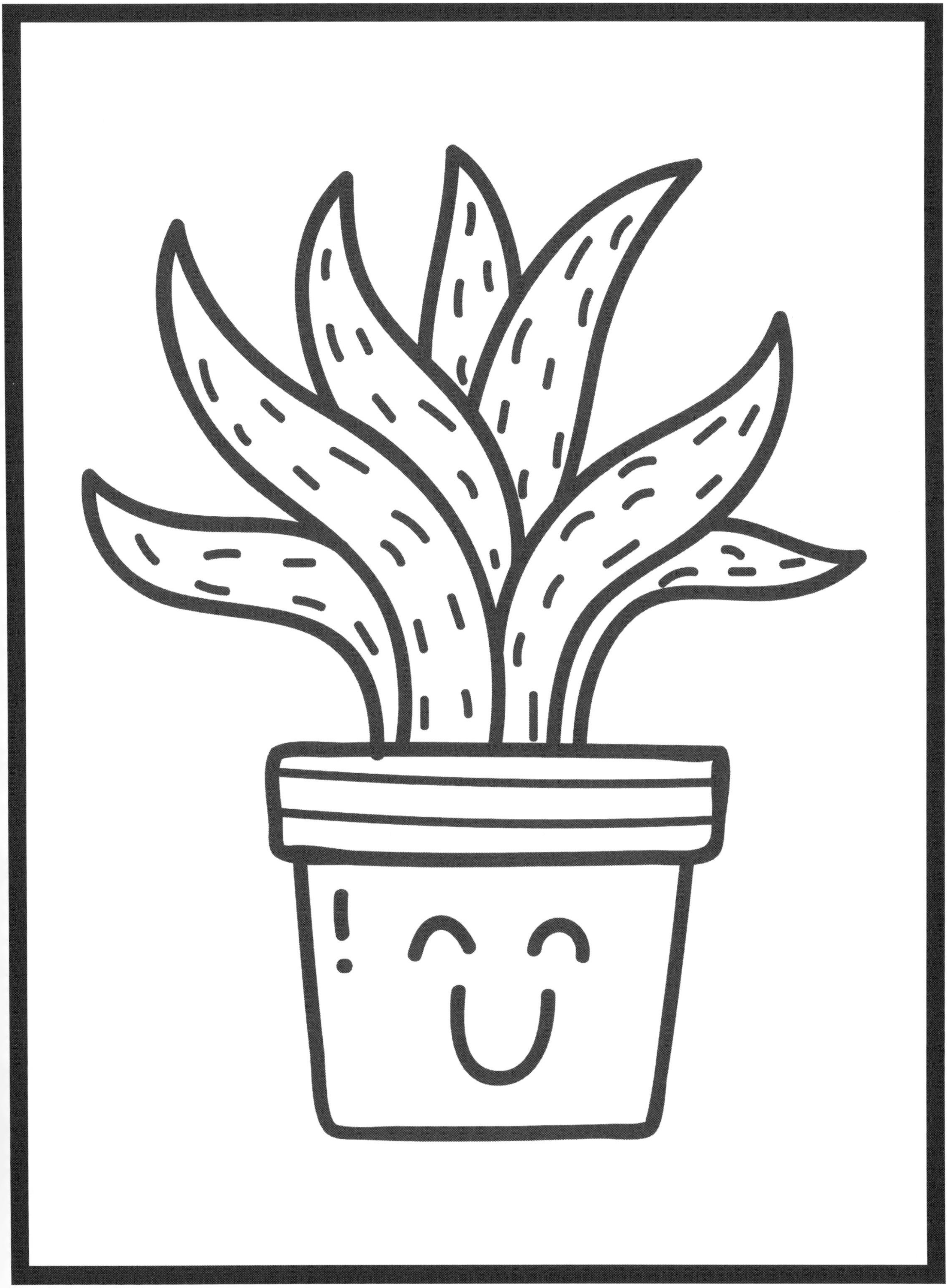

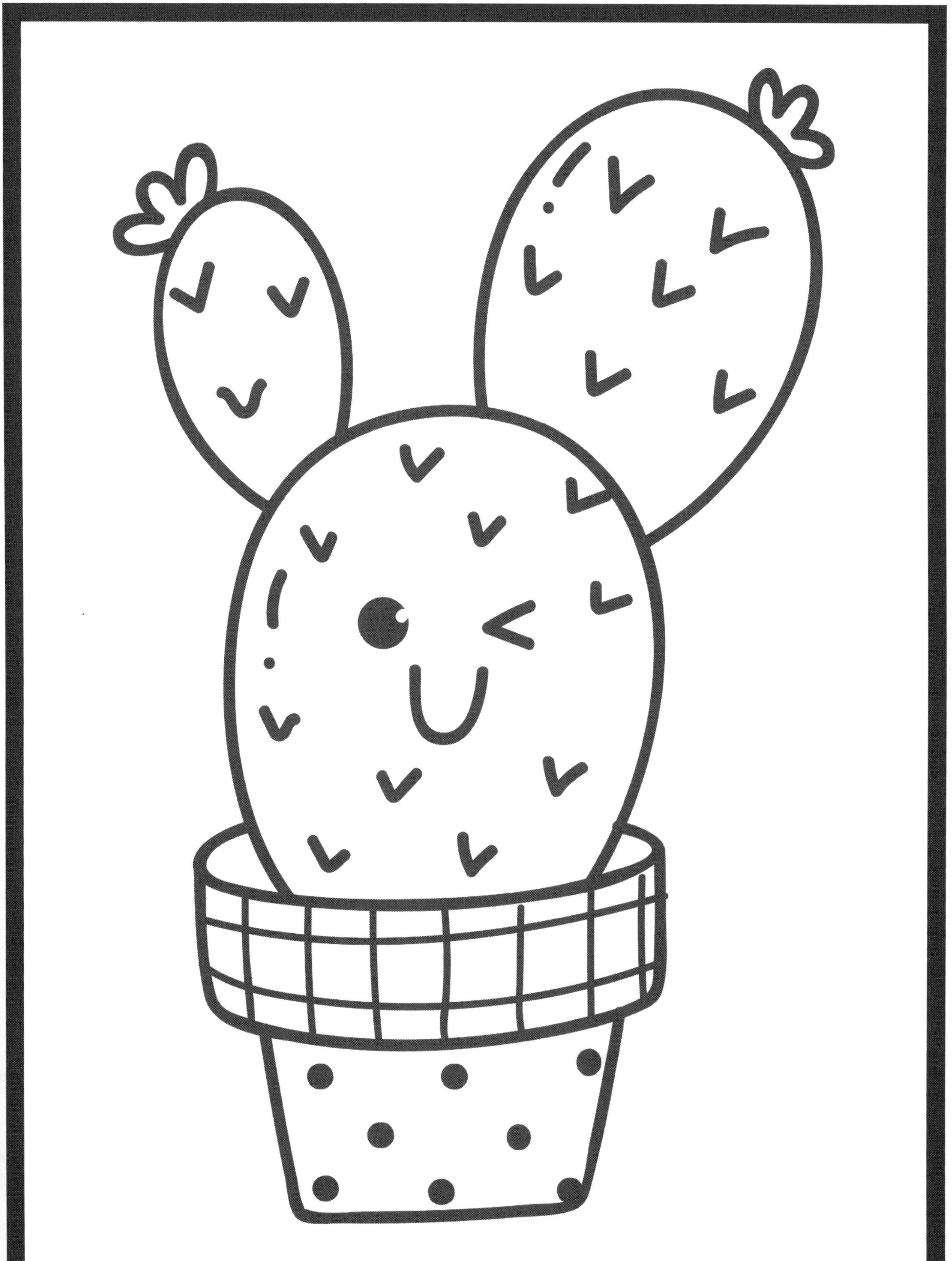

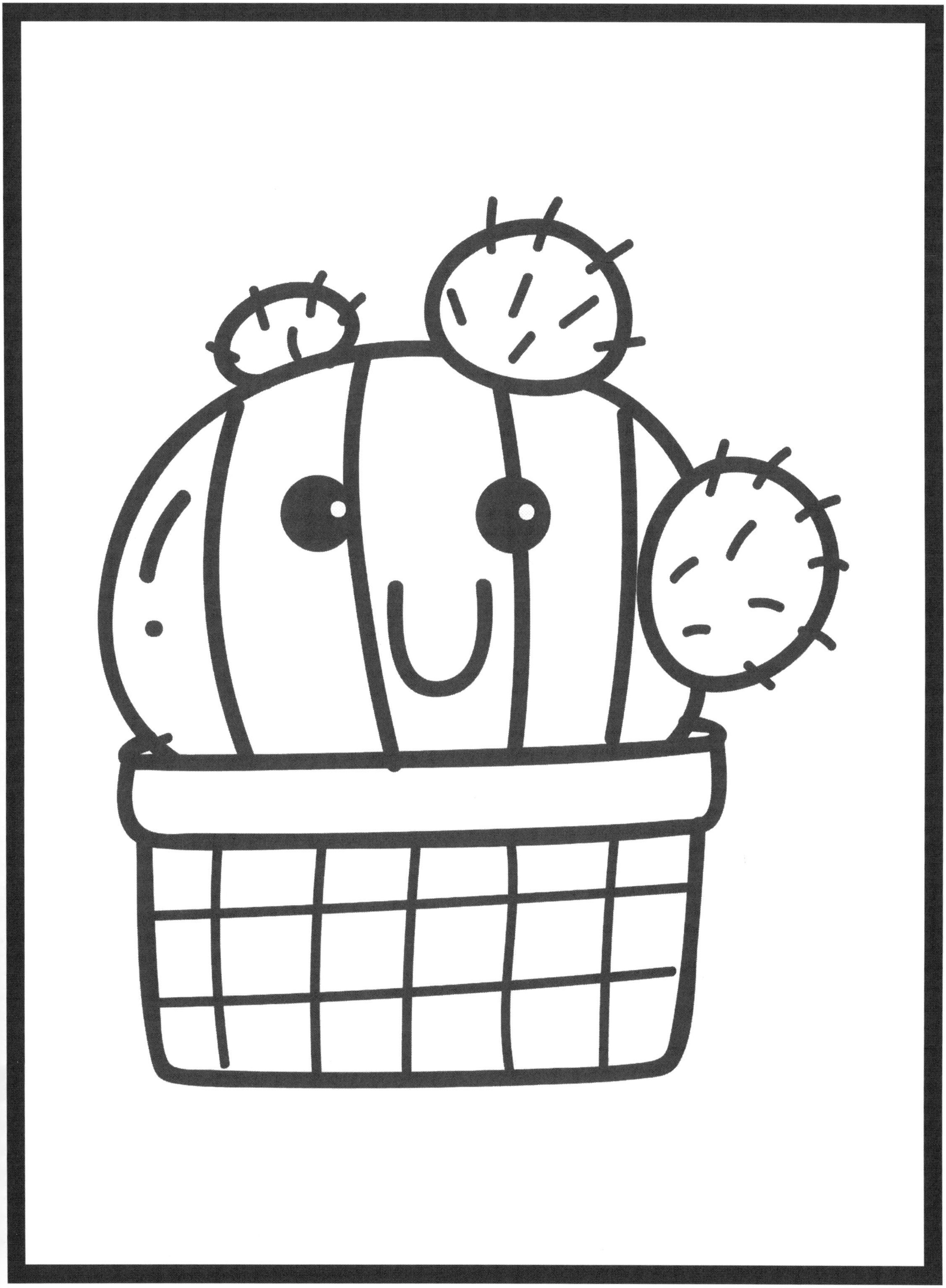

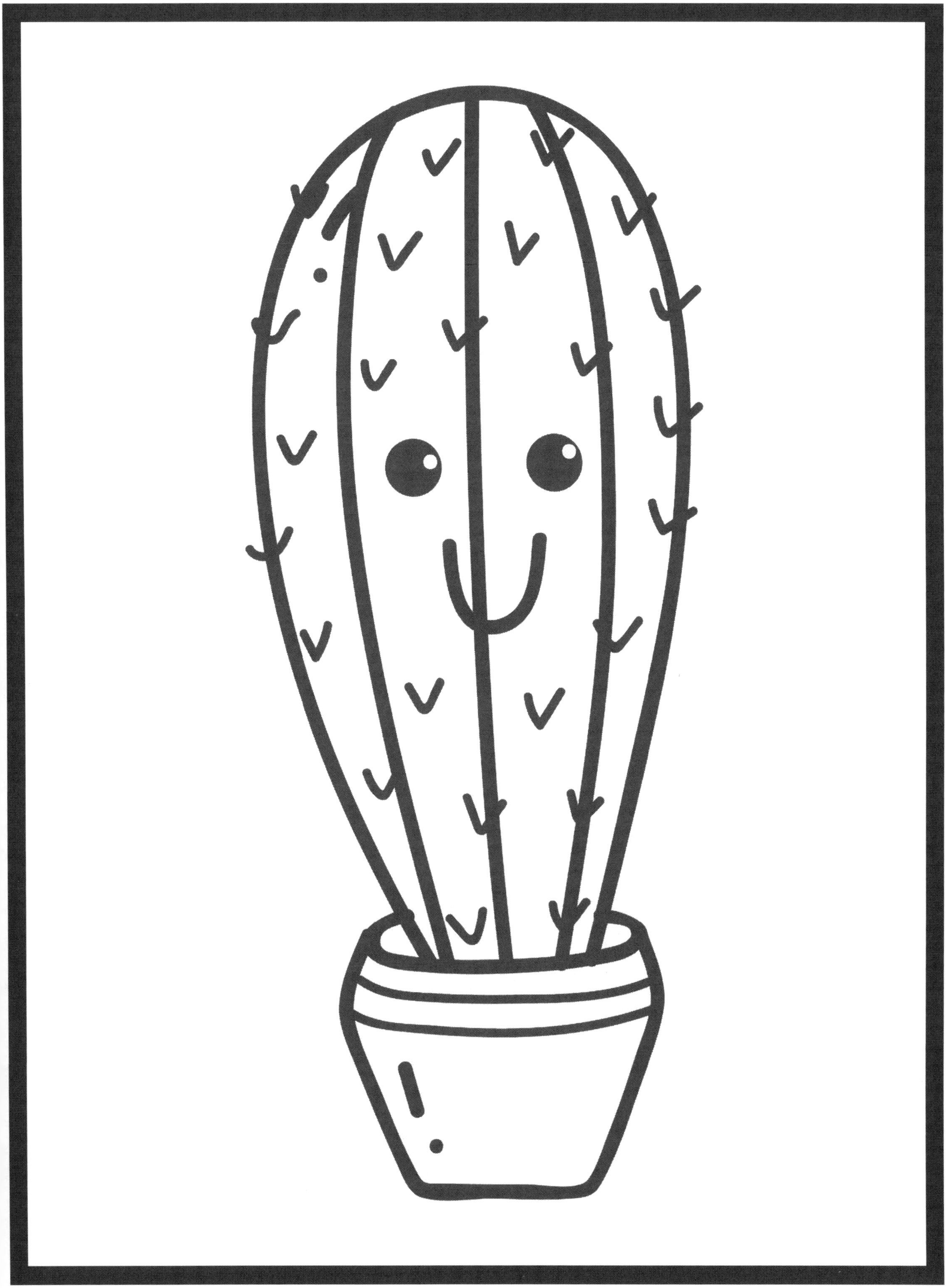

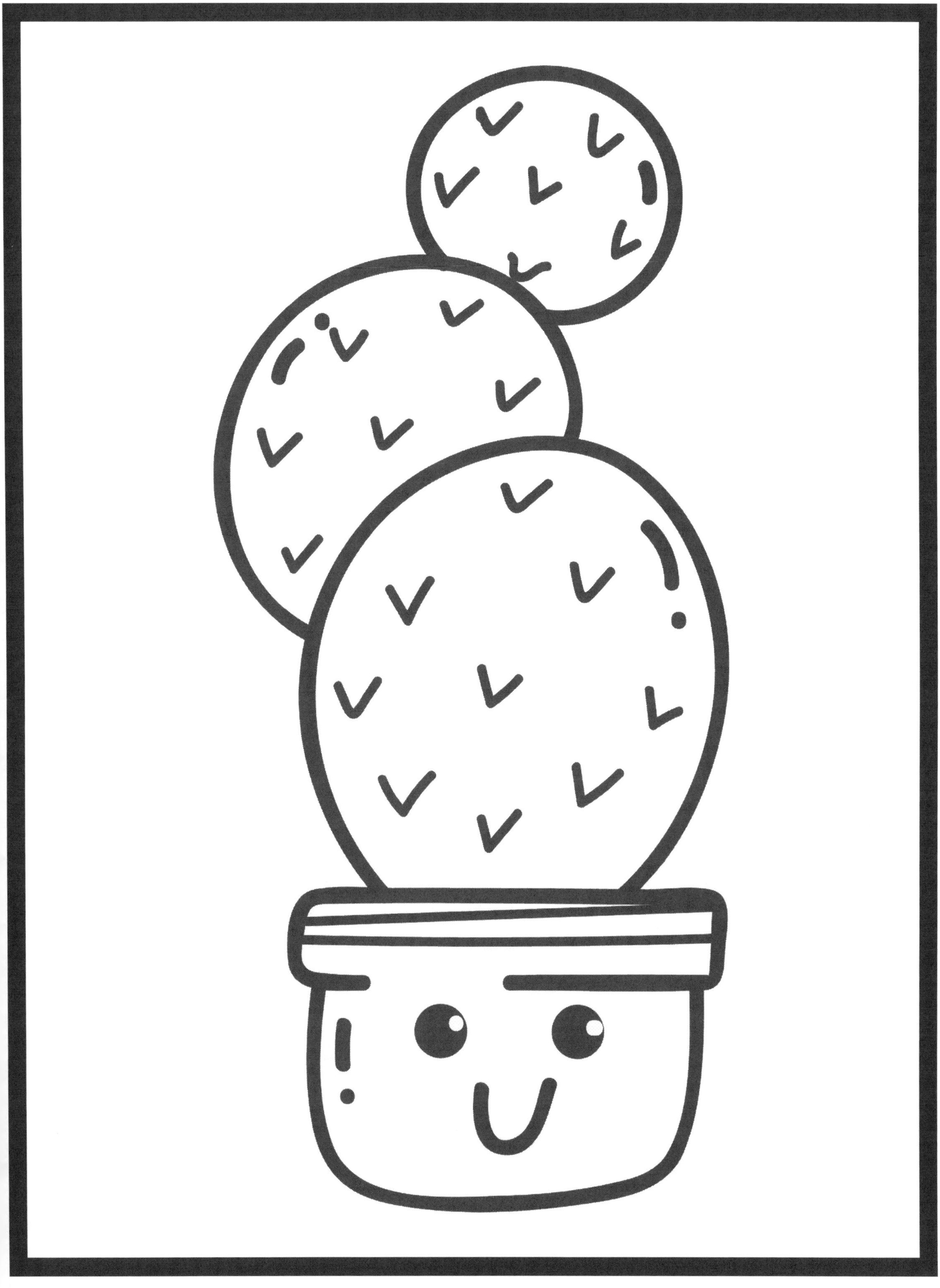

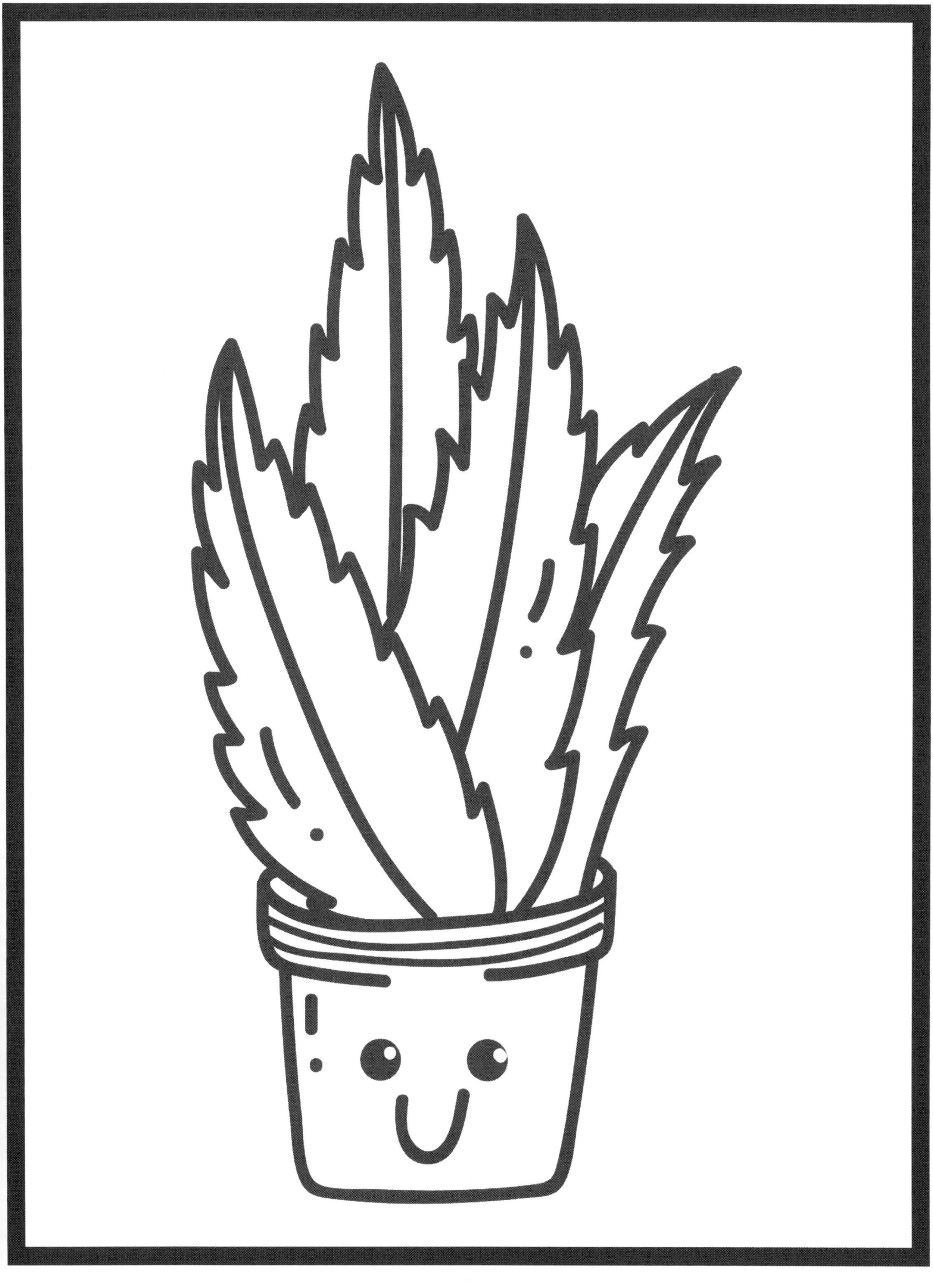

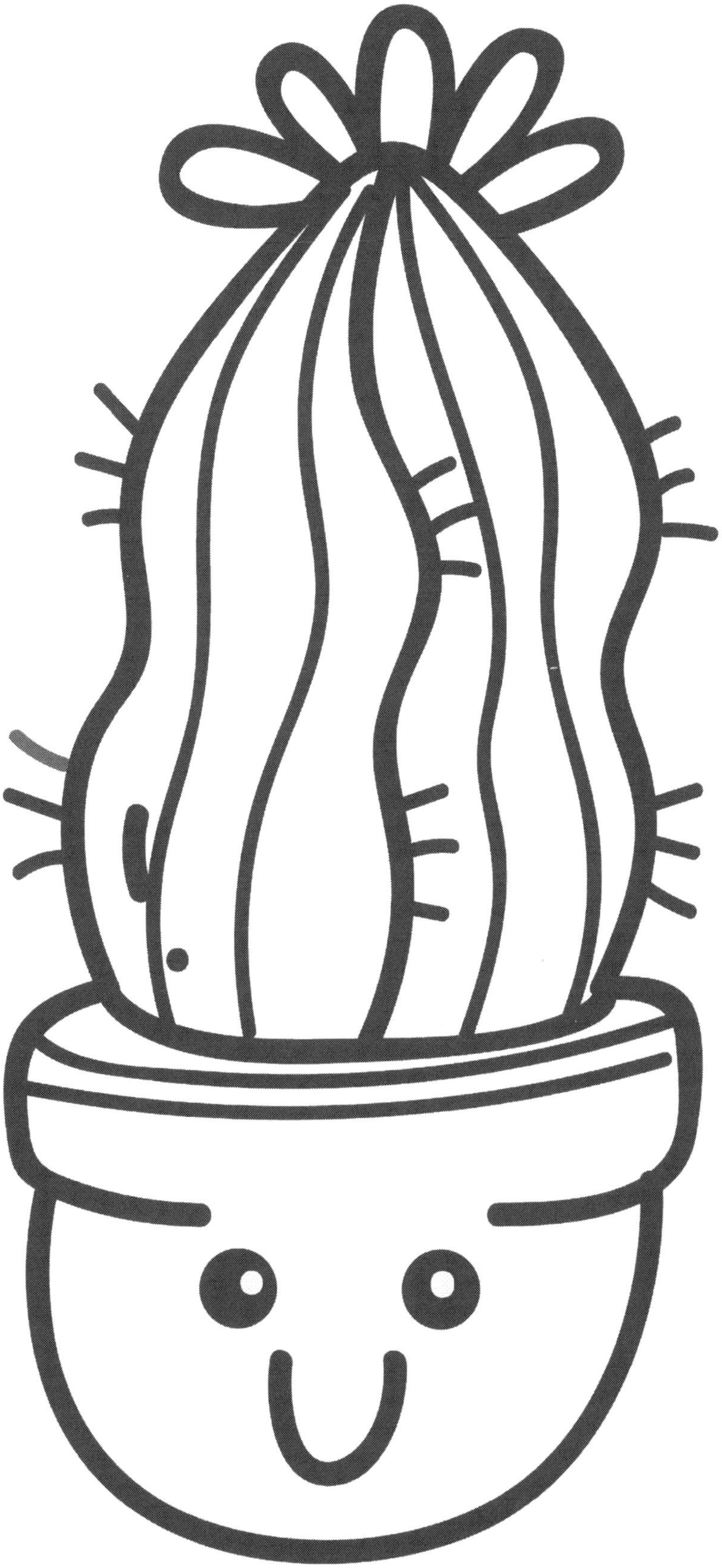

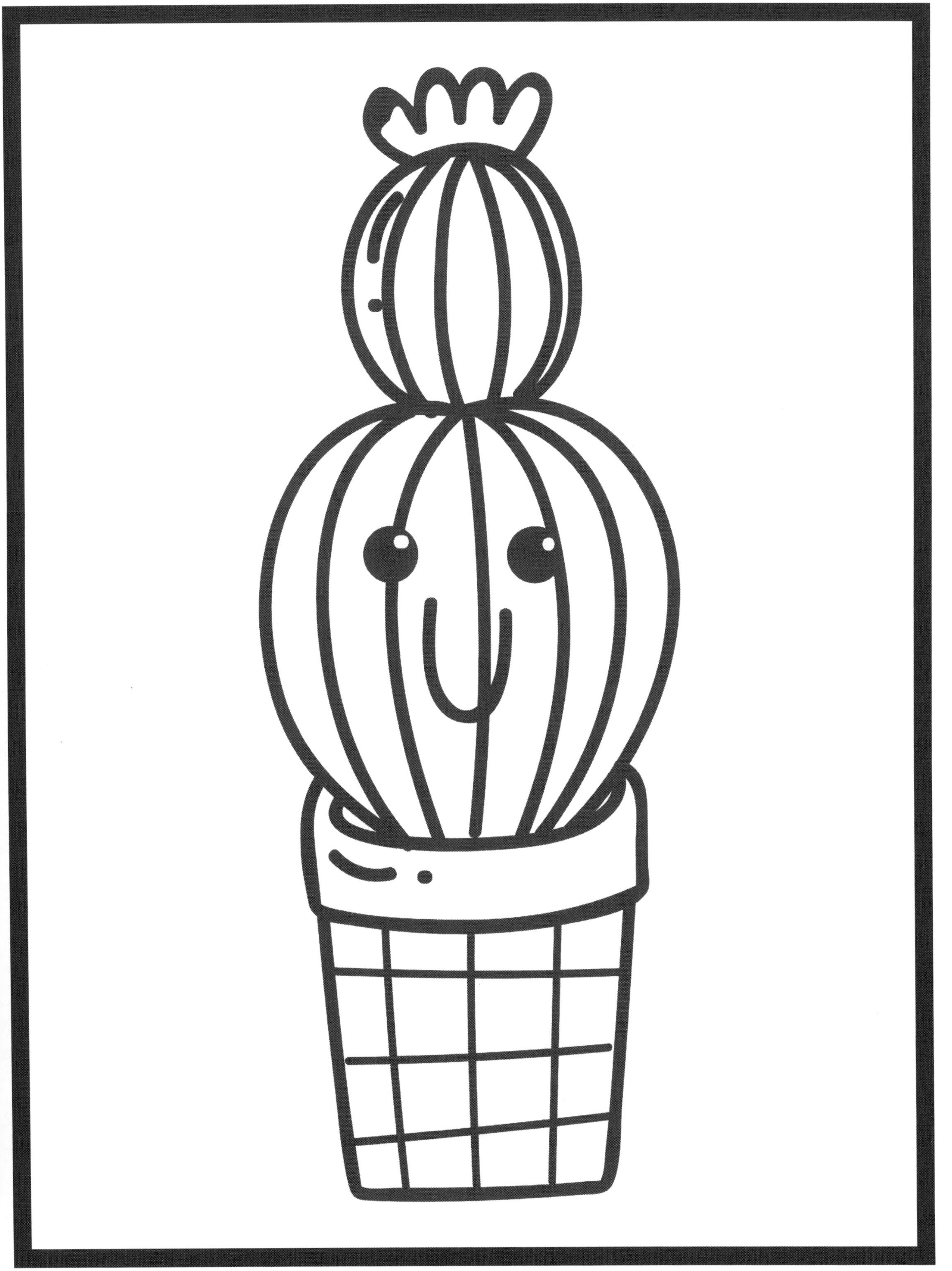

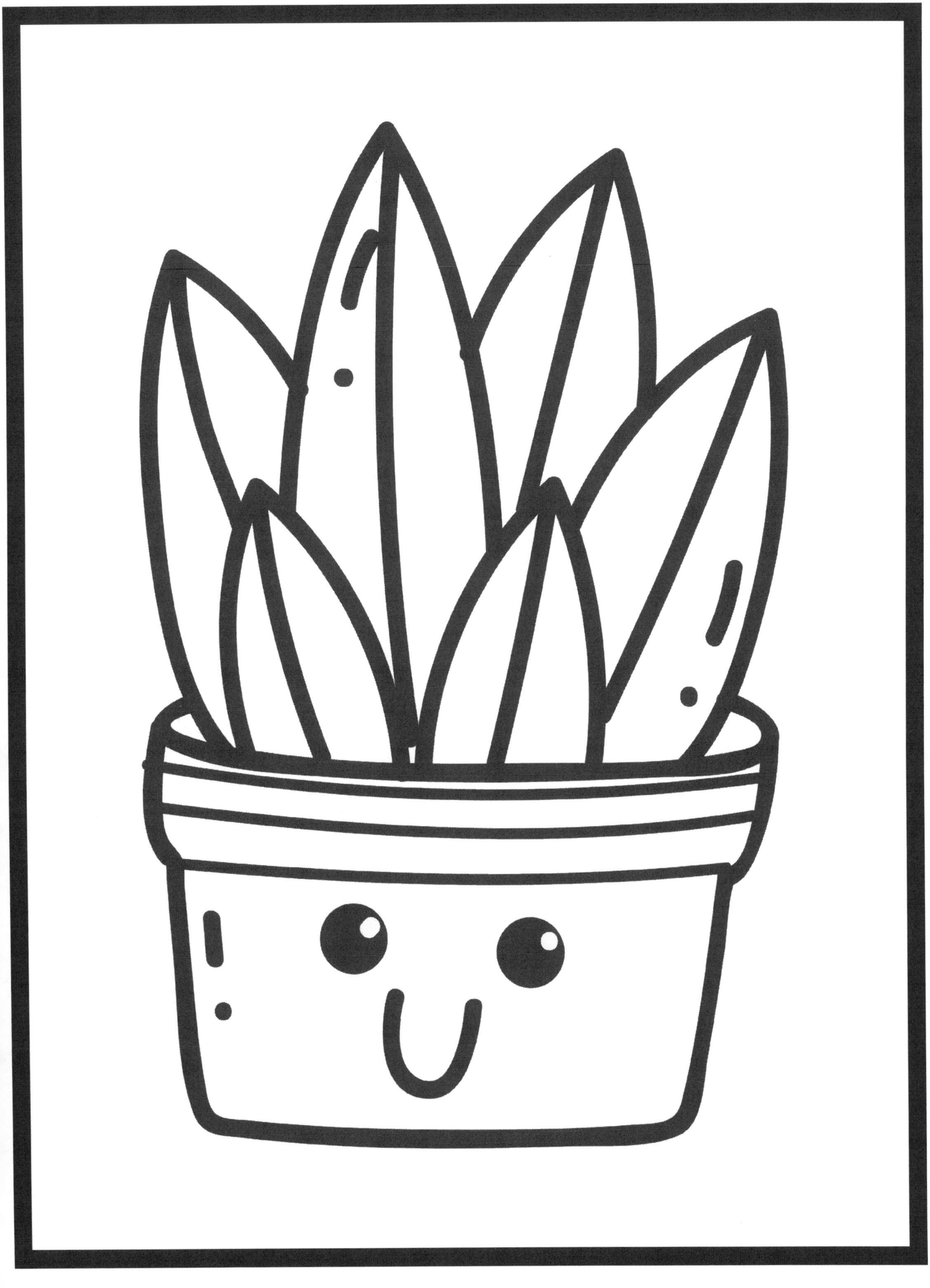

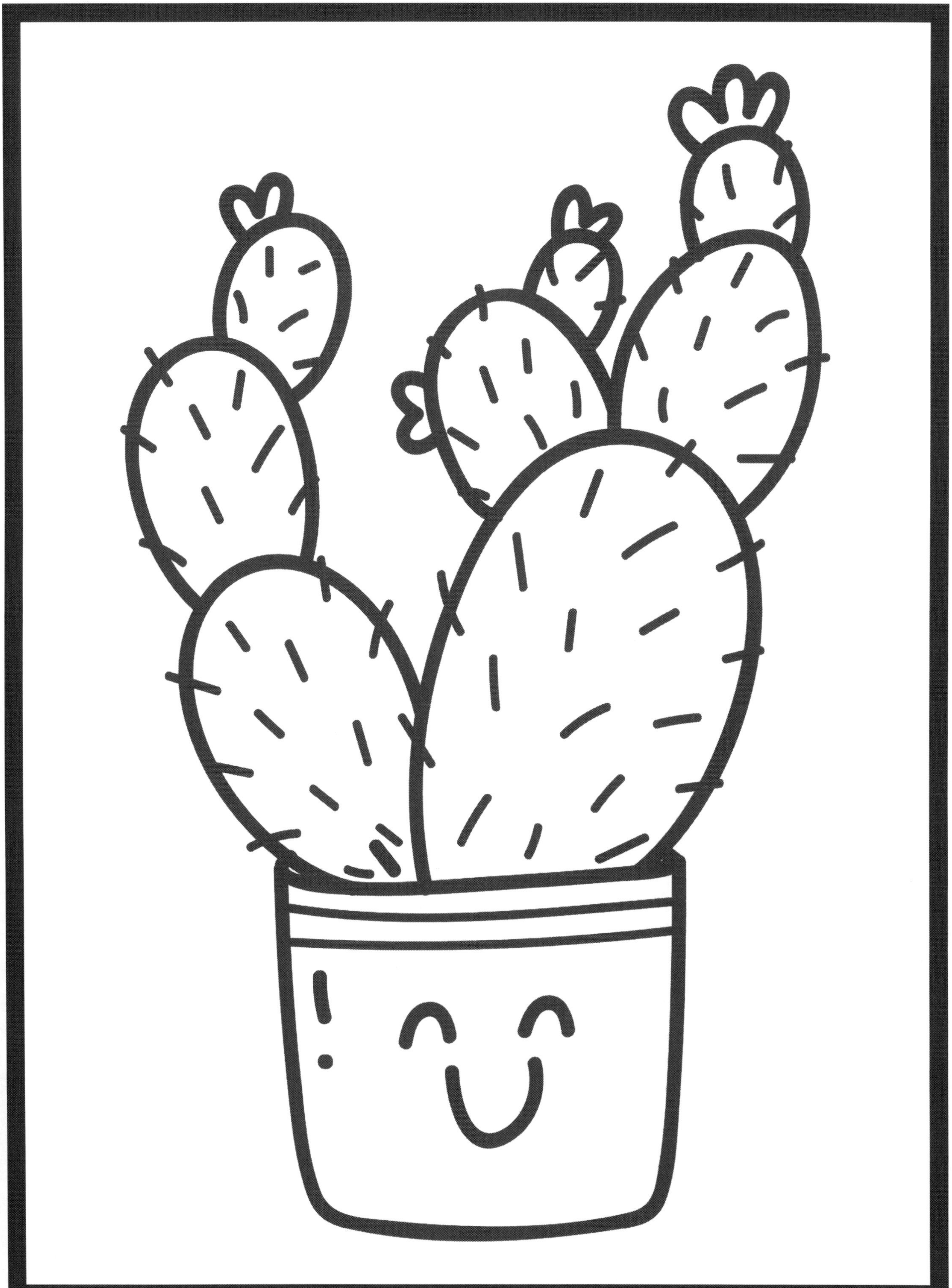

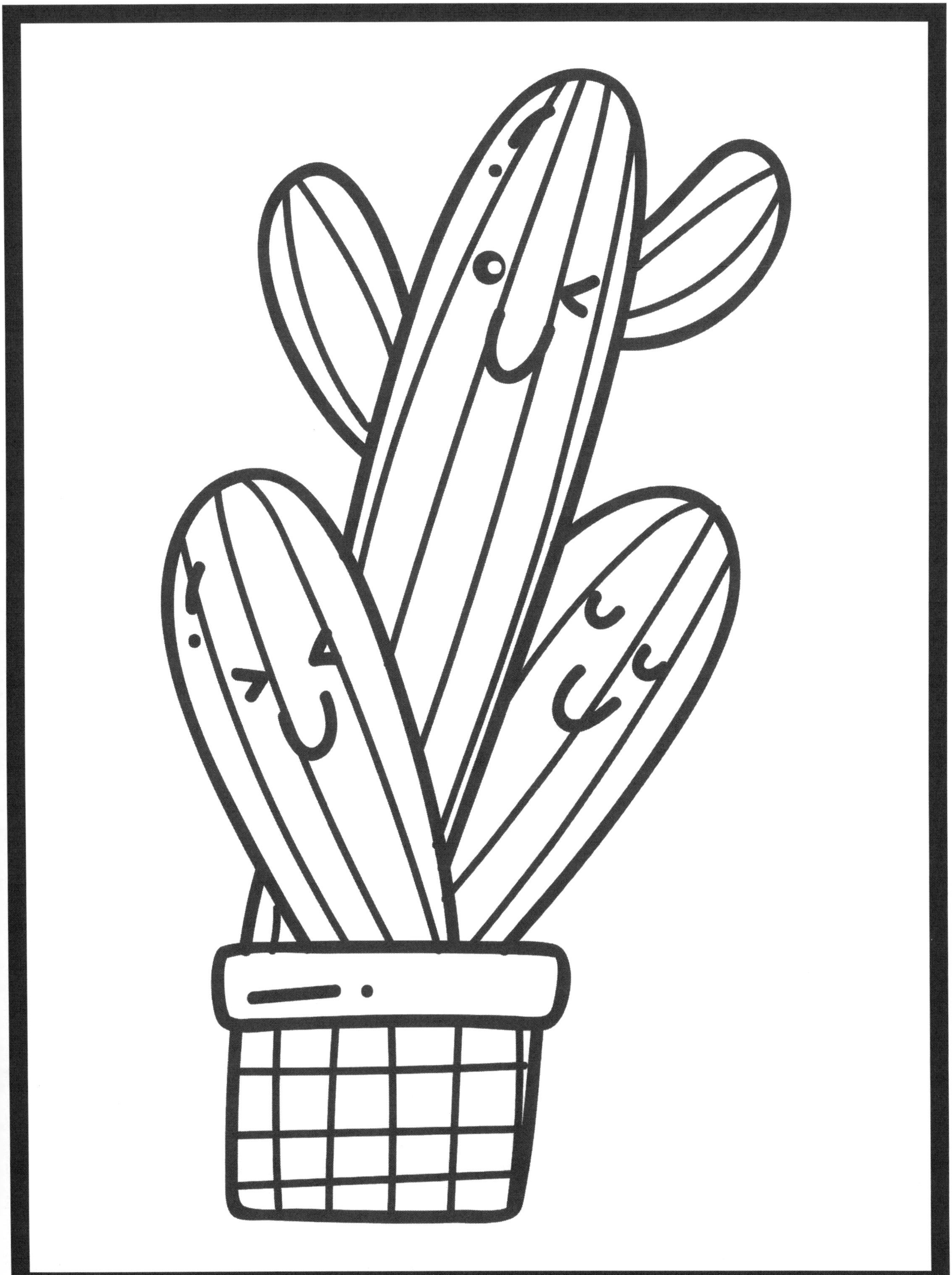

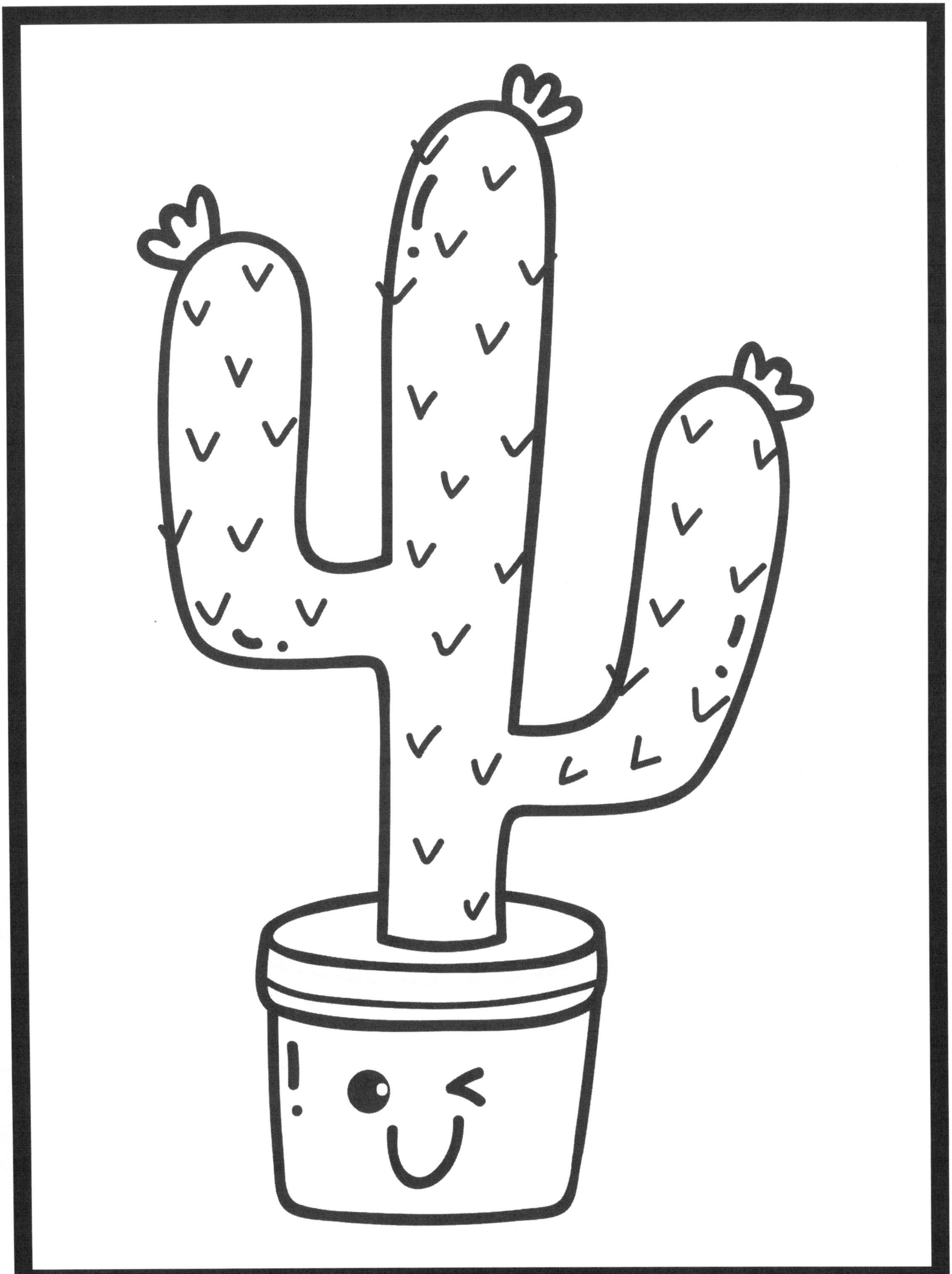

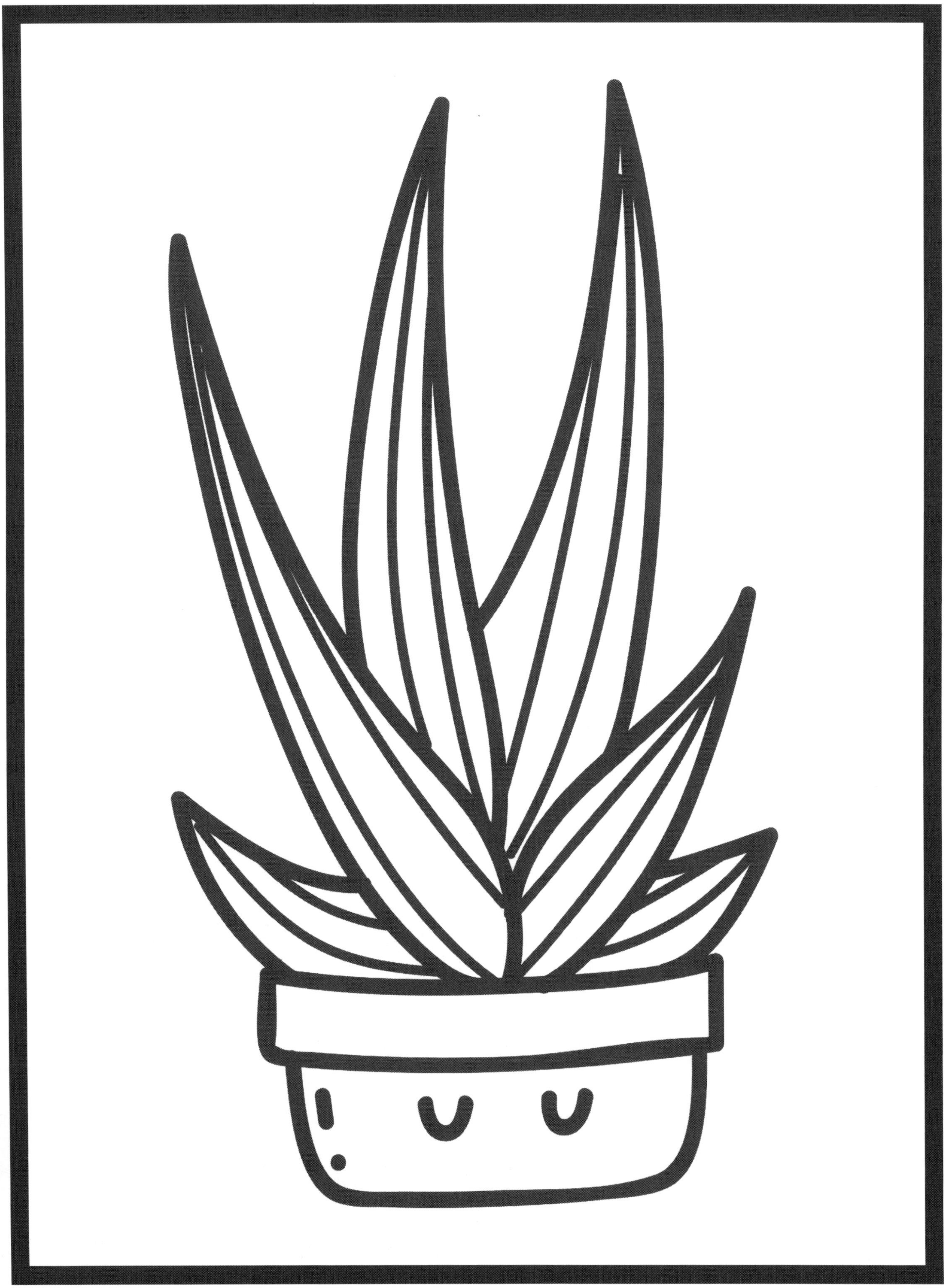

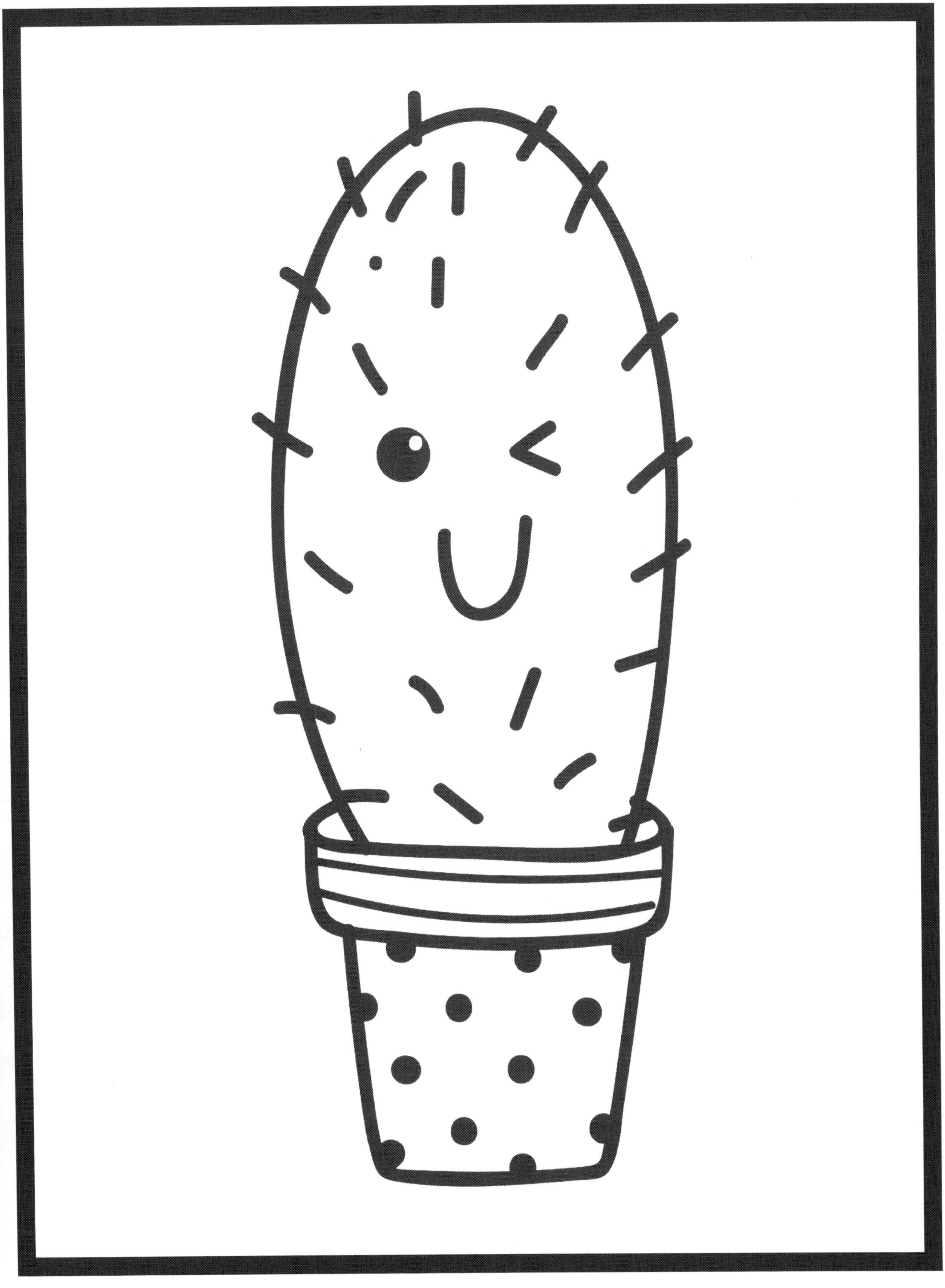

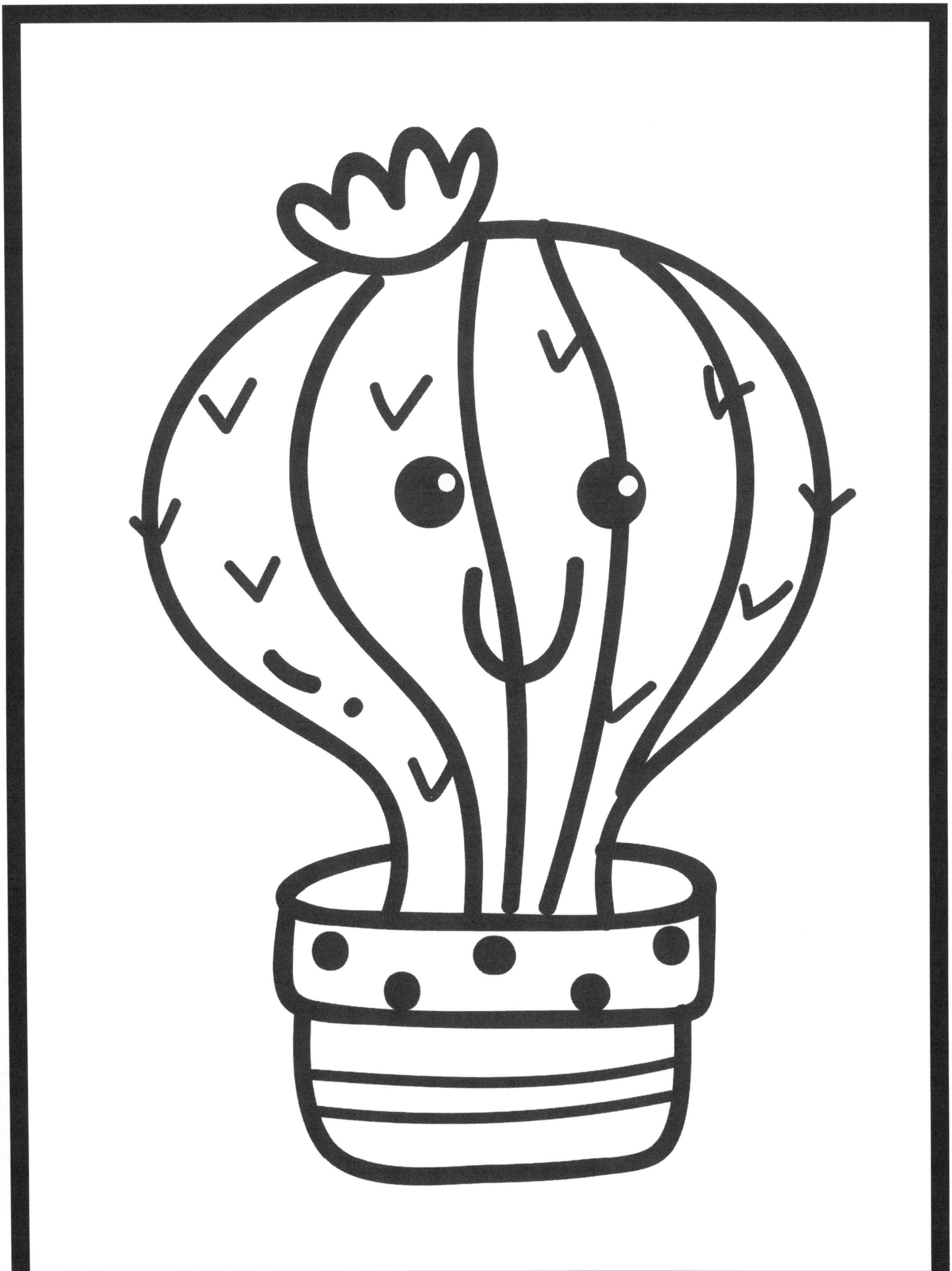

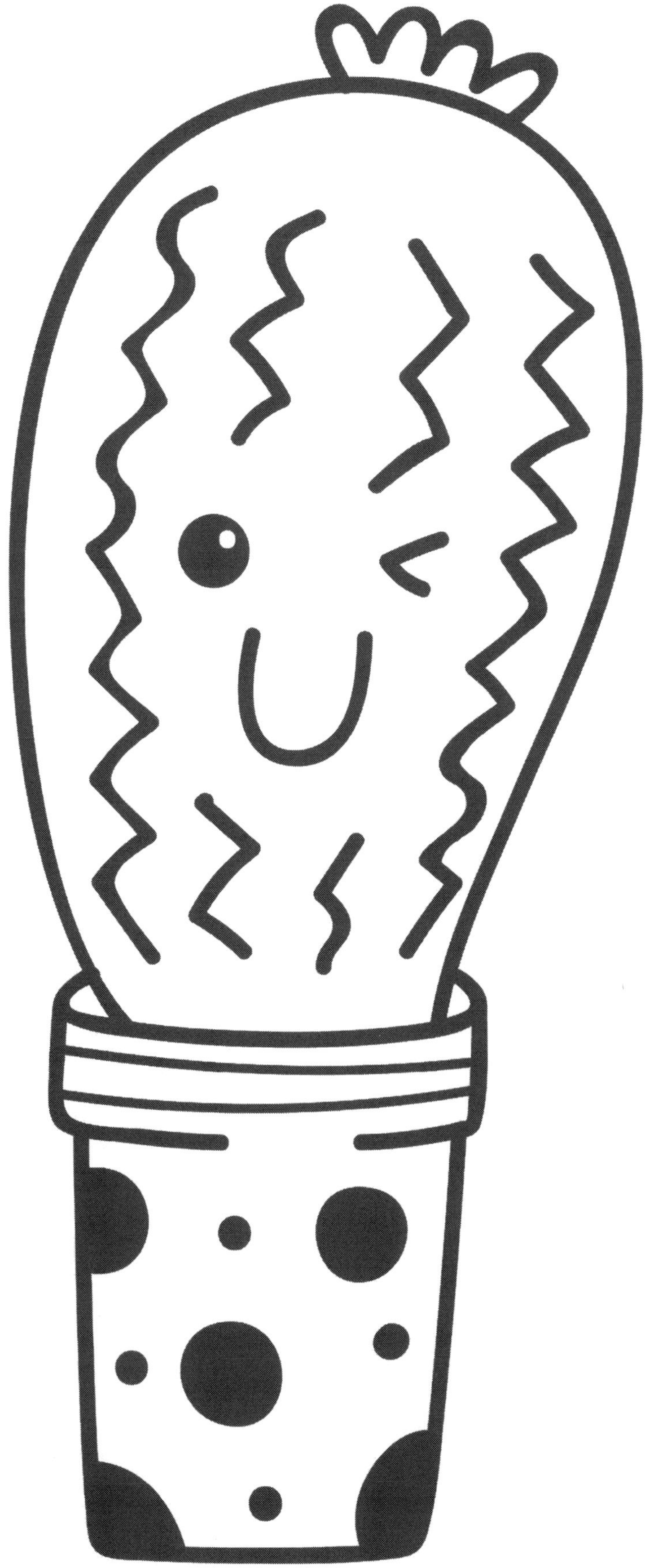

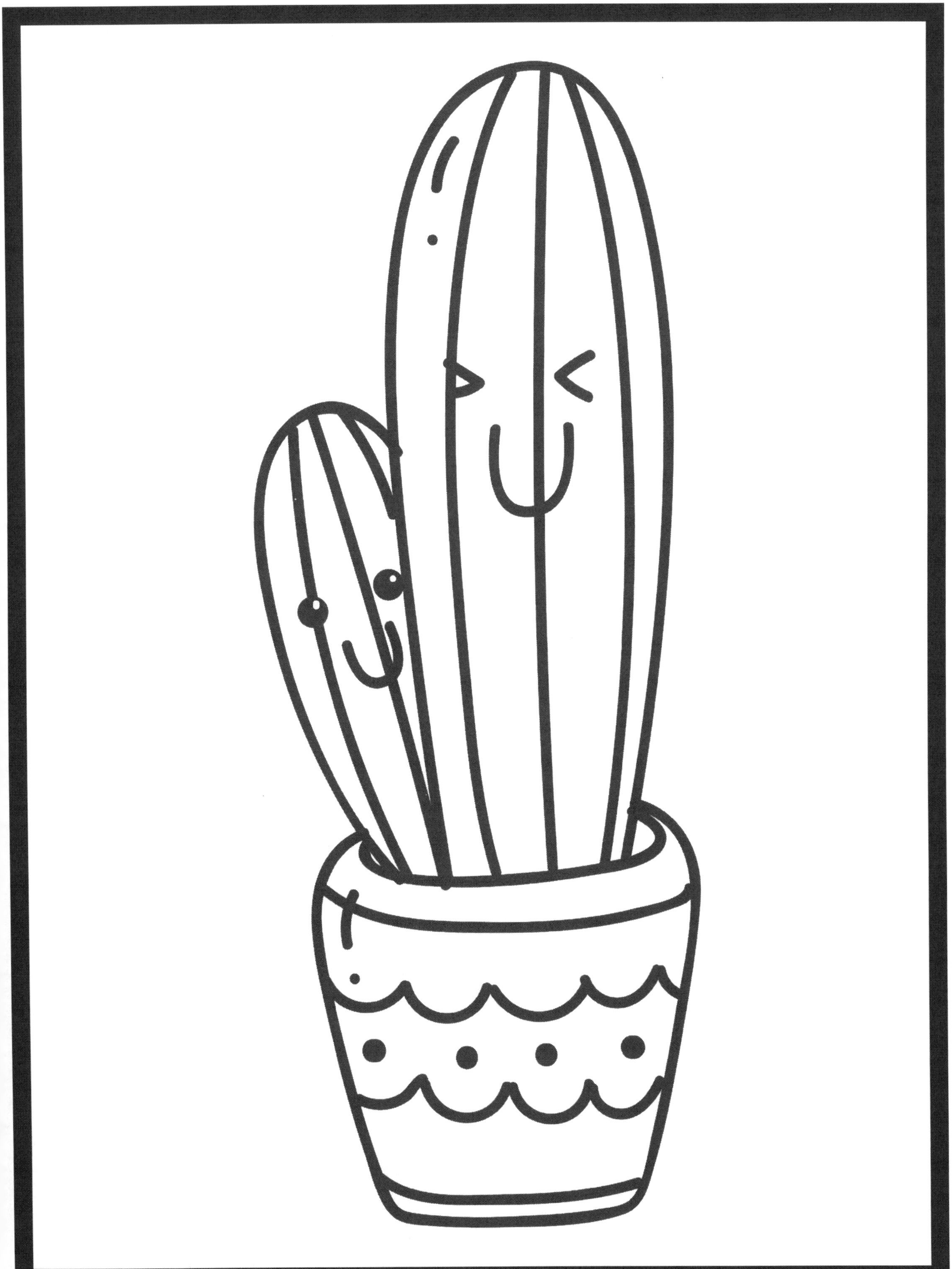

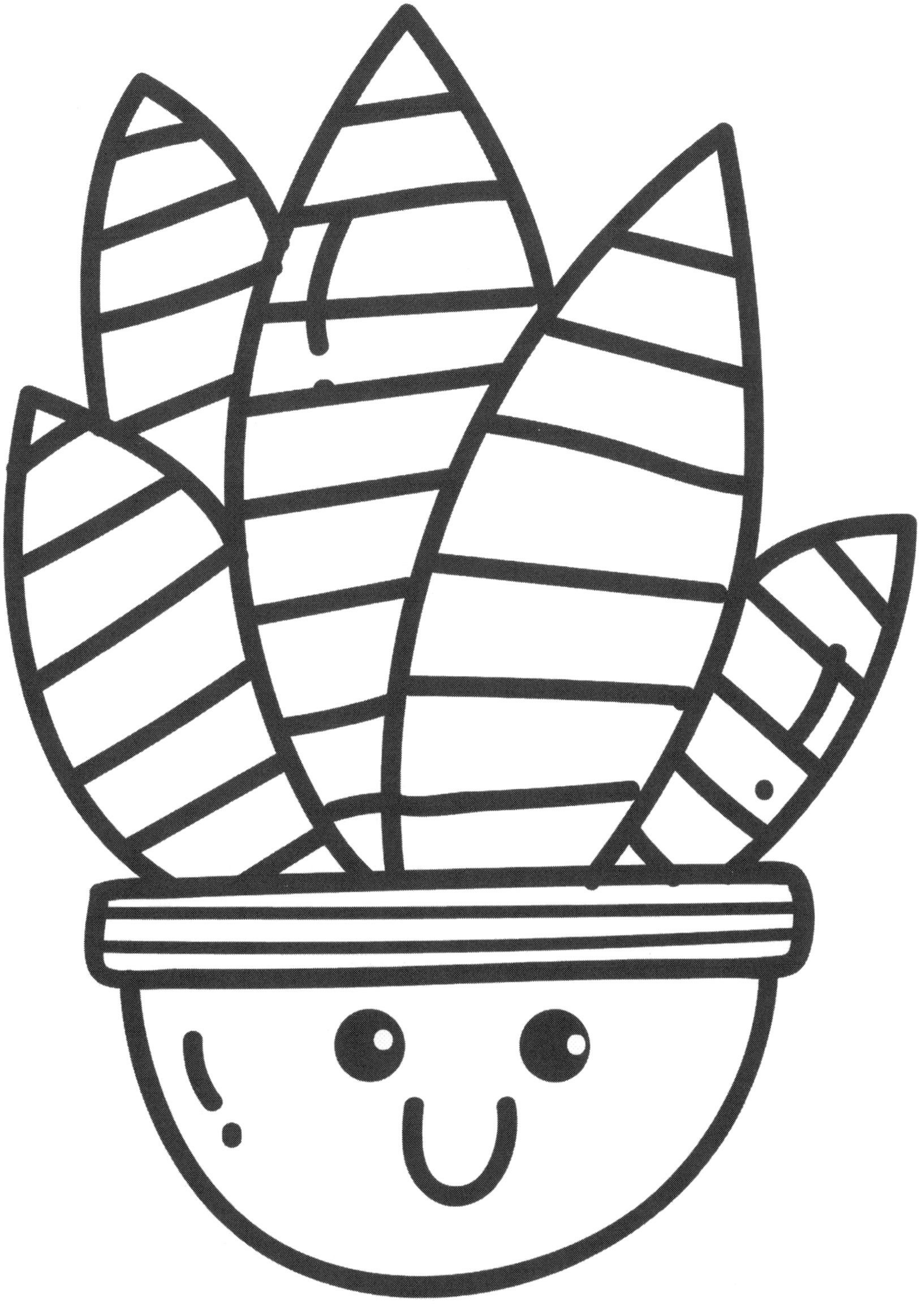

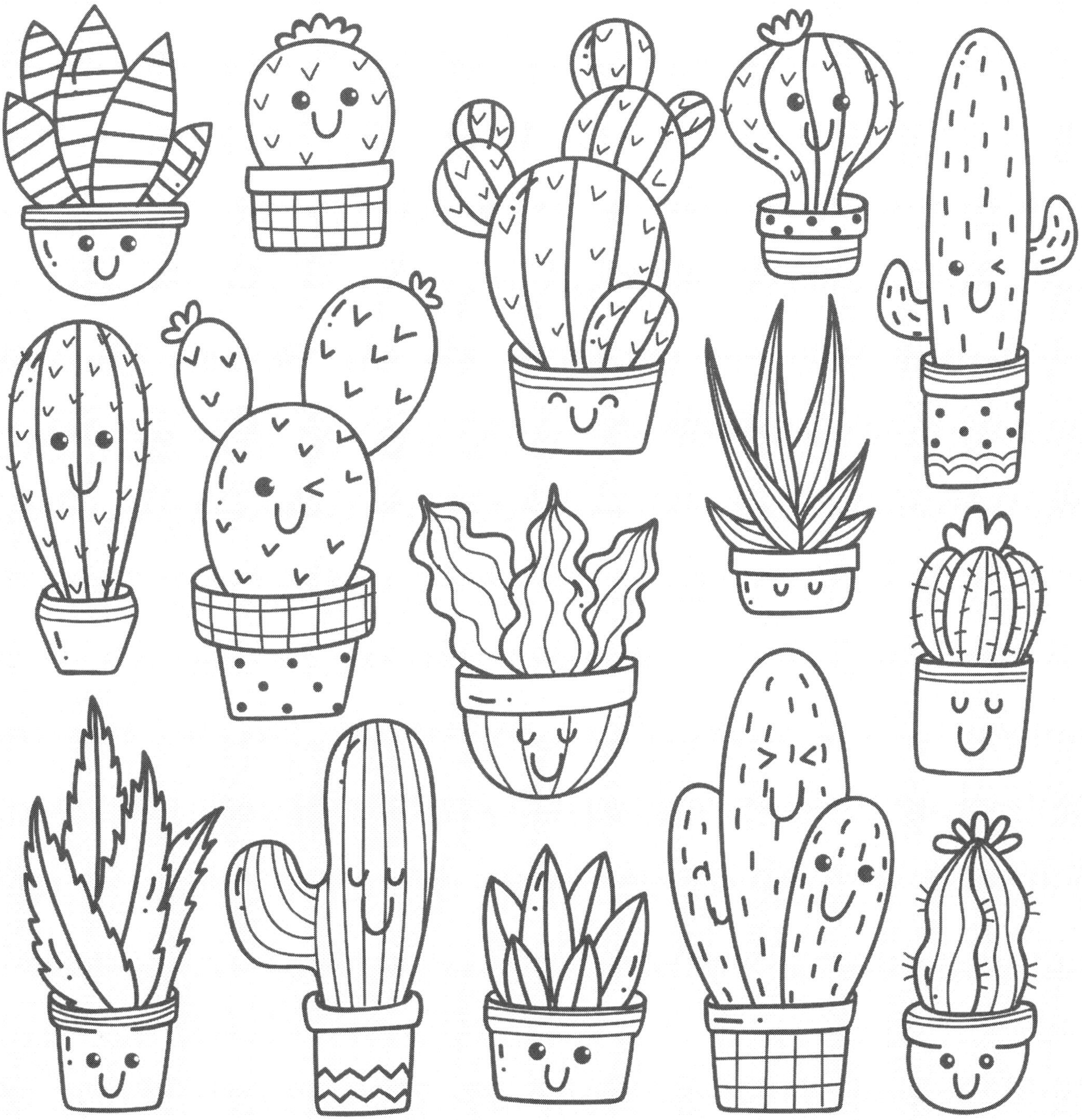

Made in the USA
Las Vegas, NV
06 February 2023

66984040R00037